Ready to Learn
Addition

How To Play

1 Press the Power button to turn the SD-X Reader on or off. The LED will light up when the SD-X Reader is on.

2 Touch the volume buttons found on this page to adjust the volume.

3 Touch words and pictures on the page to hear audio. Touch this icon to start an activity:

PLAY

4 After two minutes of inactivity, the SD-X Reader will beep and go to sleep.

5 If the batteries are low, the SD-X Reader will beep twice and the LED will start blinking. Replace the batteries by following the instructions on the next page. The SD-X Reader uses two AAA batteries.

6 To use headphones or earbuds, plug them into the headphone jack on the SD-X Reader.

Volume

Publications International, Ltd.

SD·X
INTERACTIVE

Battery Information
Includes two replaceable AAA batteries (UM-4 or LR03).

Battery Installation
1. Open battery door with small flat-head or Phillips screwdriver.
2. Install new batteries according to +/- polarity. If batteries are not installed properly, the device will not function.
3. Replace battery door; secure with small screw.

Battery Safety
Batteries must be replaced by adults only. Properly dispose of used batteries. See battery manufacturer for disposal recommendations. Do not dispose of batteries in fire; batteries may explode or leak. Do not mix alkaline, standard (carbon-zinc), or rechargeable (nickel-cadmium) batteries. Do not mix old and new batteries. Only recommended batteries of the same or equivalent type should be used. Remove weakened or dead batteries. Never short-circuit the supply terminals. Non-rechargeable batteries are not to be recharged. Do not use rechargeable batteries. If batteries are swallowed, in the USA, promptly see a doctor and have the doctor phone 1-202-625-3333 collect. In other countries, have the doctor call your local poison control center. This product uses 2 AAA batteries (2 X 1.5V = 3.0 V). Use batteries of the same or equivalent type as recommended. The supply terminals are not to be short-circuited. Batteries should be changed when sounds mix, distort, or become otherwise unintelligible as batteries weaken. The electrostatic discharge may interfere with the sound module. If this occurs, please simply restart the sound module by pressing any key.

In Europe, the dustbin symbol indicates that batteries, rechargeable batteries, button cells, battery packs, and similar materials must not be discarded in household waste. Batteries containing hazardous substances are harmful to the environment and to health. Please help to protect the environment from health risks by telling your children to dispose of batteries properly and by taking batteries to local collection points. Batteries handled in this manner are safely recycled.

Warning: Changes or modifications to this unit not expressly approved by the party responsible for compliance could void the user's authority to operate the equipment.

NOTE: This equipment has been tested and found to comply with the limits for a Class B digital device, pursuant to Part 15 of the FCC Rules. These limits are designed to provide reasonable protection against harmful interference in a residential installation. This equipment generates, uses, and can radiate radio frequency energy and, if not installed and used in accordance with the instructions, may cause harmful interference to radio communications. However, there is no guarantee that interference will not occur in a particular installation. If this equipment does cause harmful interference to radio or television reception, which can be determined by turning the equipment off and on, the user is encouraged to try to correct the interference by one or more of the following measures: Reorient or relocate the receiving antenna. Increase the separation between the equipment and receiver. Connect the equipment into an outlet on a circuit different from that to which the receiver is connected. Consult the dealer or an experienced radio TV technician for help.

Writer: Beth Goers

Cover illustrated by Olin Kidd

Illustrator: Olin Kidd

Image Sources: Image Club; Photodisc; Shutterstock

Louis Weber, C.E.O., Publications International, Ltd.
7373 North Cicero Avenue   Ground Floor, 59 Gloucester Place
Lincolnwood, Illinois 60712   London W1U 8JJ

Customer Service:
1-888-724-0144 or customer_service@pilbooks.com
www.pilbooks.com

SD-X Interactive is a registered trademark in the United States and Canada.

Manufactured in China.

8 7 6 5 4 3 2 1
ISBN-10: 1-4508-4680-7
ISBN-13: 978-1-4508-4680-6

How Many in All?

Adding is putting sets together.
You **add** to find out how many **in all**.

2 bananas + 3 more bananas is 5 bananas in all.

is ___ in all.

 4 7 5

is ___ in all.

 6 7 8

is ___ in all.

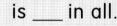 5 6 7

is ___ in all.

 7 8 9

Add It Up!

4 oranges and 3 oranges equals 7.

$$4 + 3 = 7$$

 PLAY

$2+4=6$
$2+3=6$

$3+3=7$
$3+3=6$

$4+4=7$
$4+5=9$

$8+2=10$
$2+8=9$

$1+6=8$
$1+6=7$

$9+3=12$
$3+3=6$

A **sum** is the result of adding two or more numbers. The sum tells you how many there are in all.

PLAY

6+2

4+1

1+5

1+2

2+4

5+3

9+1

8+3

2+7

5+6

1+3

7+2

1
2
3
4
5
6
7
8
9

2
+3
☐

7
+1
☐

3
+6
☐

7+1= ☐

2+3= ☐

3+6= ☐

Adding in Any Order

4 + 9 = **14** 12 13

5 + 8 = 11 **13** 16

2 + 6 = 7 9 **8**

7 + 3 = 9 **10** 11

8 + 5 = **13** 14 11

9 + 4 = 13 **13** 15

3 + 7 = 9 12 **10**

6 + 2 = **8** 10 9

Counting On

Counting on is a strategy for finding the number in all.

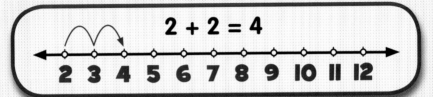

$$2 + 2 = 4$$

2 3 4 5 6 7 8 9 10 11 12

8 + 3

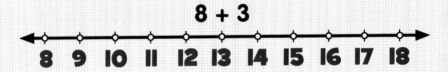

8 9 10 11 12 13 14 15 16 17 18

6 + 3

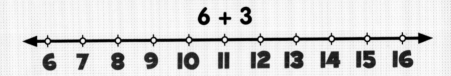

6 7 8 9 10 11 12 13 14 15 16

7 + 4

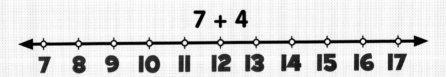

7 8 9 10 11 12 13 14 15 16 17

9 + 5

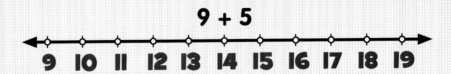

9 10 11 12 13 14 15 16 17 18 19

2 + 6

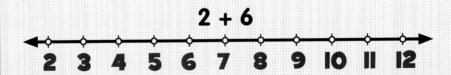

2 3 4 5 6 7 8 9 10 11 12

Finding the Missing Numbers

PLAY

5 + 1 = __	5
__ + 4 = 7	1
9 + __ = 10	6
__ + 6 = 11	3

Using an Addition Chart to Add

 PLAY

The arrows show you how to find the sum for 2 + 3.

+	1	2	3	4	5	6	7	8	9
1	2	3	4	5	6	7	8	9	10
2	3	4	5	6	7	8	9	10	11
3	4	5	6	7	8	9	10	11	12
4	5	6	7	8	9	10	11	12	13
5	6	7	8	9	10	11	12	13	14
6	7	8	9	10	11	12	13	14	15
7	8	9	10	11	12	13	14	15	16
8	9	10	11	12	13	14	15	16	17
9	10	11	12	13	14	15	16	17	18

For more practice, use your calculator!

Adding Sums to 18

7+4= ☐

$$\begin{array}{r} 5 \\ +7 \\ \hline \end{array}$$ ☐

$$\begin{array}{r} 8 \\ +3 \\ \hline \end{array}$$ ☐

9+9= ☐

5+9= ☐

$$\begin{array}{r} 6 \\ +6 \\ \hline \end{array}$$ ☐

$$\begin{array}{r} 9 \\ +8 \\ \hline \end{array}$$ ☐

4+7= ☐

6+4= ☐

$$\begin{array}{r} 7 \\ +9 \\ \hline \end{array}$$ ☐

1
2
3
4
5
6
7
8
9
10
11
12
13
14
15
16
17
18

Making Half

When a **whole** unit is cut into two equal pieces, each piece is called a **half**.

Making Fourths

When a whole unit is cut into four equal pieces, each piece is called a **fourth**.

Making Thirds

When a whole unit is cut into three equal pieces, each piece is called a **third**.

Fractions

Fractions are numbers that describe part of a whole thing. A fraction has a top number and a bottom number.

The top number tells how many parts you have. → $\dfrac{1}{2}$

The bottom number tells how many parts make up the whole.

PLAY

Groups of 10

Sets of 10	Ones left over
2	

Sets of 10	Ones left over
	6

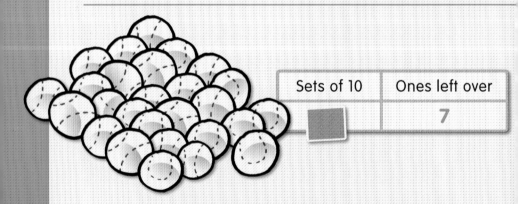

Sets of 10	Ones left over
	7

1 2 3 4 5 6 7 8 9

Sets of 10	Ones left over

Sets of 10	Ones left over

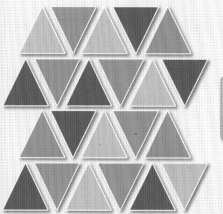

Sets of 10	Ones left over

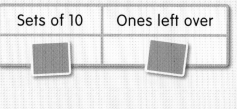

Tens and Ones

tens	ones	
4	2	42 = 4 tens + 2 ones

65 = 6 tens + 5 ones
65 = 5 tens + 6 ones

47 = 4 tens + 6 ones
47 = 4 tens + 7 ones

29 = 9 tens + 2 ones
29 = 2 tens + 9 ones

83 = 8 tens + 3 ones
83 = 8 tens + 4 ones

51 = 5 tens + 1 one
51 = 6 tens + 1 one

42

Adding 3 Numbers

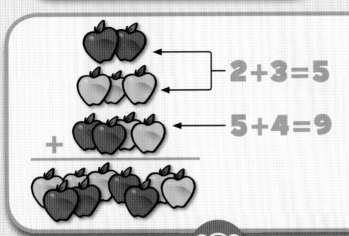

$$2+3=5$$

$$5+4=9$$

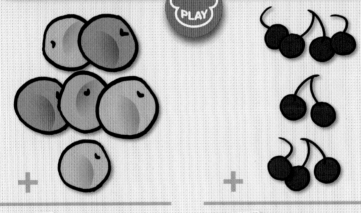

| 6 | 4 | 7 |

| 11 | 9 | 12 |

Adding 2-Digit and 1-Digit Numbers

PLAY

67
28
38
18
93
19
59
29
47
76
88
39

12
+6
_____

24
+5
_____

81
+7
_____

63
+4
_____

36
+2
_____

92
+1
_____

51
+8
_____

17
+2
_____

73
+3
_____

22
+6
_____

44
+3
_____

31
+8
_____

Adding Two
2-Digit Numbers

Add the ones first. Then add the tens.

$$\begin{array}{r} 42 \\ +21 \\ \hline 3 \end{array} \qquad \begin{array}{r} 42 \\ +21 \\ \hline 63 \end{array}$$

$$\begin{array}{r} 32 \\ +11 \\ \hline \end{array} \qquad \begin{array}{r} 25 \\ +13 \\ \hline \end{array} \qquad \begin{array}{r} 22 \\ +40 \\ \hline \end{array} \qquad \begin{array}{r} 16 \\ +41 \\ \hline \end{array} \qquad \begin{array}{r} 54 \\ +23 \\ \hline \end{array}$$

45	38	55	35	77
43	28	60	57	78
39	22	62	53	68

$$\begin{array}{r} 61 \\ +10 \\ \hline \end{array} \qquad \begin{array}{r} 43 \\ +43 \\ \hline \end{array} \qquad \begin{array}{r} 80 \\ +12 \\ \hline \end{array} \qquad \begin{array}{r} 28 \\ +21 \\ \hline \end{array} \qquad \begin{array}{r} 41 \\ +34 \\ \hline \end{array}$$

66	86	93	49	75
71	77	92	50	66
77	83	82	47	82

At the Store

A penny is 1¢. A nickel is 5¢.

A dime is 10¢. A quarter is 25¢.

75¢

15¢

20¢

3¢

50¢

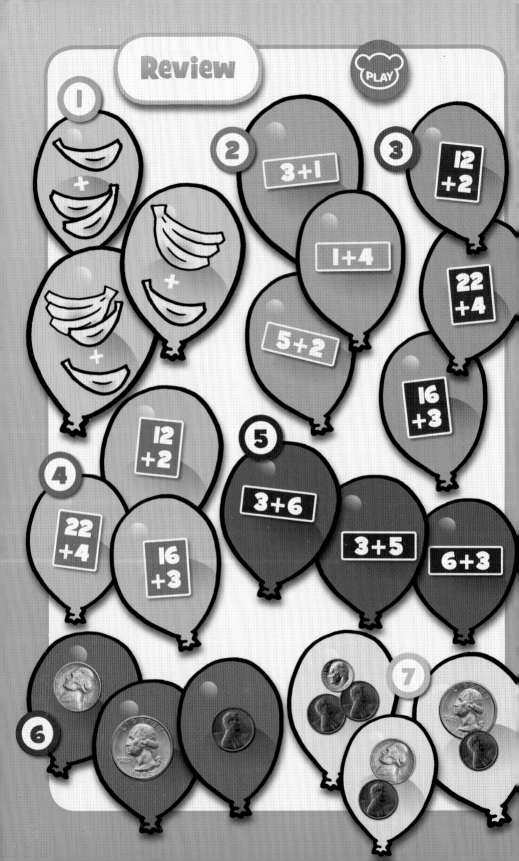

Review

PLAY

1

2 3+1

3 12
   +2

1+4

5+2

22
+4

16
+3

12
+2

4 22
   +4

16
+3

5 3+6

3+5

6+3

6

7